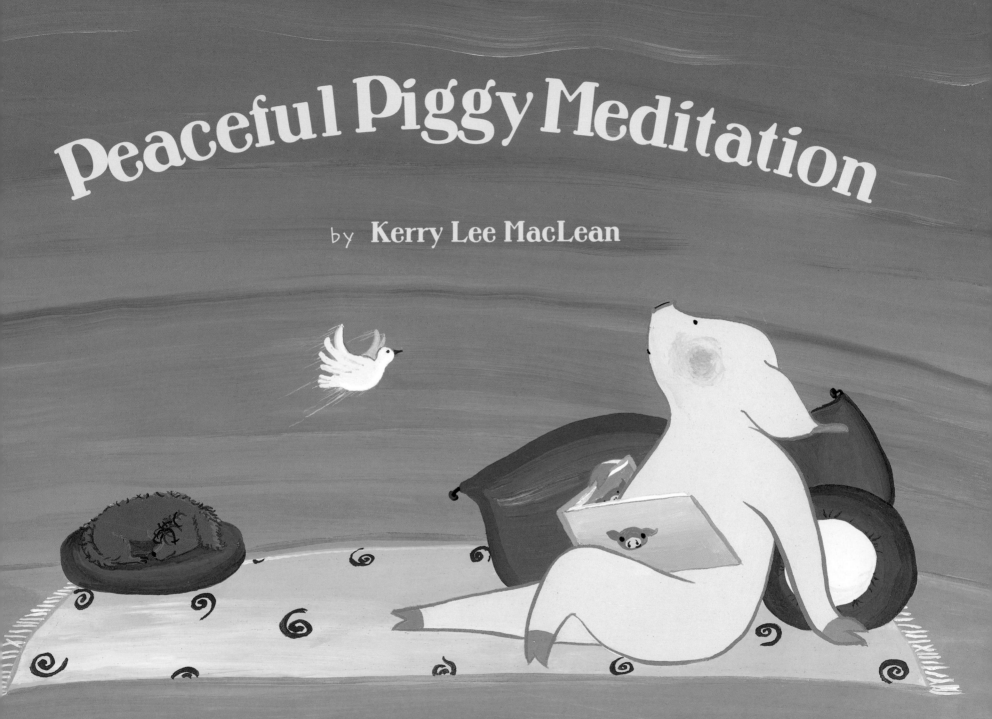

Peaceful Piggy Meditation

by Kerry Lee MacLean

Albert Whitman & Company, Morton Grove, Illinois

Dedicated to my sweet daughter, Tessa,
Queen of Loving Kindness.

My deepest gratitude goes to my meditation teacher, Mipham Rinpoche, as well as to my editors, especially Wendy McClure. Extra-special thanks to Acharyas Judith Simmer-Brown and Reggie Ray, my daughters, Sophie and Tessa Maclaren and Kelly MacLean, all of whom worked tirelessly.
Many remarkable people kindly gave their insights, encouragement, and energy to this project: Hector, Gregory, and Andrew MacLean; Amy, Kazmo, and Dhyana Kida; Leland Williams; Caroline Bartholow; Norah Murray; Gina Otto; Jewel Duncan; Elaine, Rick, Nick, and Natalie Pease; Maud Roehr; Alicia Fordham; and the entire 2003 Boulder Rites of Passage class. Thank you!

Library of Congress Cataloging–in–Publication Data

MacLean, Kerry Lee.
Peaceful piggy meditation / written and illustrated by Kerry Lee MacLean.
p. cm.
Summary: Peaceful pigs demonstrate the many benefits of meditation.
ISBN 0–8075–6380–3 (hardcover)
[1. Meditation—Fiction. 2. Pigs—Fiction.] I. Title.
PZ7.M22436Pi 2004   [Fic]—dc22   2004000526

Text and illustrations copyright © 2004 by Kerry Lee MacLean.
Published in 2004 by Albert Whitman & Company,
6340 Oakton Street, Morton Grove, Illinois 60053–2723.
Published simultaneously in Canada by Fitzhenry & Whiteside, Markham, Ontario.
10 9 8 7 6 5 4 3 2 1

For more information about Albert Whitman & Company, visit our web site at www.albertwhitman.com.

Please visit the author's web site at: www.kerryleemaclean.com.

Sometimes the world can be such a
busy, noisy place.

RING!

Oinkers' School

Welcome

Sometimes it feels like you *always* have
to hurry, **hurry, hurry . . .**

and you feel like you can't **slow down.**

Even when you're **sitting down!**

It can be hard **not** to **lose**
your **temper** when
you're **angry**

and you can get **really frustrated** when things don't go **your way.**

Peaceful piggies know when to take a break,

find a quiet spot and just breathe, breathe, breathe.

Mom or Dad might help them set up a **special place** with a few things . . .

maybe a crystal, for clear thinking,

a stone, for stillness,

or even a flower, for **kindness.**

Peaceful piggies sit like a king or queen on their throne, feeling the solid earth beneath them and the big sky all around them.

Every day, they sit feeling their breath going **in** and **out** until their minds **calm down**.

So, peaceful piggies feel free like a bird in the sky,

and as **calm** as a pond on a **cool, clear** night.

This makes it easier to **accept things** that happen and **stop wishing** for things to be **different**.

Come back to life, Goldie!

She's gone.

When you're **peaceful,**
you can be **truly fearless!**

Best of all, when you're feeling peaceful,
you like who you are, just as you are.

I'd better say sorry. I was mean to her.

So, it's easier to face the truth about yourself . . .

and it's easier to stand **up**

to **others**.

Peaceful piggies take **good care** of their friends . . .

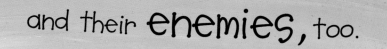

and their **enemies**, too.

They try to be **loving** and **kind** to **all beings** . . .

even worms.

By **slowing down,** peaceful piggies notice all the magical little things in life, like the way raindrops race each other down the window . . .

The way the **clouds** tell **silent** stories . . .

and the way birds sing songs just for you.

Having a **peaceful place inside** helps keep a **happy heart happy,** so that even on a **horrible . . .**

painful . . .

disgustingly **rotten** day,

a **peaceful piggy** can . . .

Peaceful Piggy Meditation

Find a quiet place to sit on the floor. Use a pillow to sit on.

Sit like the piggies: cross-legged, with a straight back, looking down at the ground about two feet in front of you.

Ring a gong or a bell to start. (If you don't have either, a metal mixing bowl makes a nice sound when you strike it with a pencil.)

As you breathe, feel the cool air coming into your nose, then feel the warmed-up air going out of your nose. If it helps, count the breaths—one in, two out, three in . . .

Feel your thoughts and emotions settling down as you sit still. If you feel yourself start thinking, thinking, thinking again, slow down. Remember to let your thoughts go, and just feel the air going in and out, in and out.

You can do this for as long as ten minutes. It may seem hard at first, but do it as long as you can—long enough to feel peaceful.

After ten minutes, ring the gong to end. Don't move yet. Wait until you can't hear the gong anymore. Enjoy the moment.

Remember this quiet feeling. Imagine that you keep it deep inside yourself all day long.

☆ Mind-in-a-Jar Experiment ☆

Before you meditate, fill a glass jar with water. Look at it and think of how it's like your mind during a quiet moment—clean and clear, like the sky.

Now take a little bit of sand or soil that you've brought in from outside and dump it in the jar. Each tiny grain is one of your thoughts. Some are happy thoughts, some are sad, some are exciting wishes, some are dark and angry feelings.

Put a lid on the jar and shake it up, so that everything swirls around, faster and faster. This is your mind in a hurry.

Now, let everything calm down by letting the jar sit still on a table. This is your mind during meditation.

Watch the thoughts settle down to the bottom, leaving the water—your mind—light and clear, instead of dark and muddy. Now you can act peacefully, because you can think clearly!

About Family Meditation

Can you imagine an entire family getting up fifteen minutes early just to practice peacefully being together for ten minutes a day? Now imagine what it would be like for a child to carry that experience with him for the rest of the day. Meditation is a lifelong discipline that, when practiced daily, soothes the mind and calms the emotions, giving both children and adults an invaluable still point within.

My husband and I raised five children while leading a hectic city life, so it was only through desperation that we first began making time to meditate with our kids regularly. It started as an emergency measure to help them through a terrible family crisis, but gradually we began to catch on to the fact that our children were just generally nicer people when they meditated every day. It may be hard to believe that stopping to meditate together just a few minutes each day could possibly make your kids happier and more peaceful and confident, but give it a try for three months and see for yourself. I saw it in my own children, and I see it all the time in the families I work with as a children's meditation teacher.

Looking back, some of our sweetest memories come from those sessions. Sometimes our kids loved the quiet time together and other times they resisted it, but they began to understand it as a self-care regimen. "You brush your teeth to keep them clean and healthy; you meditate to keep your mind happy and healthy," we explained, and they accepted it as such, growing into cheerful young adults who willingly brush their teeth and love meditating on their own.

Kerry Lee MacLean
Certified Children's Meditation Instructor
Colorado Shambhala Children's Rites of Passage Program Director